The Impromptu Speaker's Toolkit

Frameworks for Confident Communication

Jason Rosette

Copyright © 2024 Jason Rosette

linktr.ee/businessvoicecoach

All rights reserved

ISBN (kdp): 9798329164787

CONTENTS

	Introduction	i
2	Introducing: PREP & TREET	Pg. 1
3	*Practice:* PREP & TREET Questions and Responses	Pg. 23
4	Recap	Pg. 37
5	Action Steps for the Emerging Speaker	Pg. 41
6	Conclusion	Pg. 44
7	About the Author	Pg. 46

INTRODUCTION

Picture this: I was leading a workshop for a group of high-level executives when, out of the blue, a hand rose up from the back of the room. "Mr. Rosette," a stern-looking C-suite type intoned, "How would you handle a situation where a major client suddenly announces they're pulling their business?"

The room fell silent, and all eyes were on me. I knew I had to say something compelling, but didn't want to start off with any hedging words or phrases (ala, 'that's a great question'). For a moment, I felt that familiar panic – the dreaded "deer in the headlights" sensation.

But then I instinctively homed in on my impromptu speaking frameworks, and chose a suitable one to make my response. I took a slow, even breath, and began.

I acknowledged the CEO's concern, then stated my point. I provided a reason with some supporting data, then outlined a few suggested key steps for managing the situation, using one of the impromptu speaking templates I will be sharing with you here today.

After concluding, I offered to follow up later with a more detailed plan. By the time I finished speaking, the tension in the room had eased, and the CEO seemed satisfied with my answer.

That experience taught me a valuable lesson: even the most seasoned communicators can be caught off guard by impromptu speaking challenges. But with the right tools and preparation, it's possible to overcome the initial panic and deliver a clear, concise, and compelling message. That's what I hope to share with you in this book.

Hi, I'm Jason Rosette, a communication consultant working in a range of media and public speaking sectors over the past three decades.

I began my communications journey as a filmmaker over three decades ago, then expanded from there into performing arts, including the vocal arts. Eventually, I found that my director-performer background had broad application in public speaking areas, which I utilize when coaching clients with aspects of their public speaking performance.

Now I happen to view public speaking as a 'cousin' of the more widely known performing arts, and I'll dig into this performative aspect in greater detail at another time.

In this resource, I'm presenting a walk-through of a pair of **impromptu speaking** frameworks which I've found to be incredibly useful for myself and my public speaking clients. What is impromptu speaking? **Impromptu speaking is the art of delivering a**

speech or presentation with little to no preparation. It requires an ability to think and process on your feet, to organize your thoughts quickly, and to communicate effectively under pressure.

Impromptu speaking is, in my view, more challenging than prepared speaking due to the fact that advance preparation is limited, or even absent. A speaker therefore needs a starting point, or framework, in order to present effectively in an impromptu way.

Consider the following frameworks to be like tools in a toolbox, each with its own strength and optimal application depending on the situation and environment. Together, these popular core frameworks help individuals navigate spontaneous speaking situations with confidence and clarity.

In my role, I've had the privilege of working with diverse clients from around the world, each with their own unique communication challenges. Whether it's a professional transitioning into a more communication-centric role or a startup entrepreneur looking to refine their pitch, the need for effective impromptu speaking skills is universal.

Most of my clients come to me with a specific need, usually based upon a recent 'inciting incident' (to use screenwriter terminology). There is often a specific change in a client's career which demands that they enhance their public speaking skills.

Based on responses from my standard client intake

form, I often see that the clients' inciting incident is usually something along the lines of: a) a recent job promotion into an area which requires more public speaking and presenting, and/or b) a memorable past instance of a poorly executed impromptu presentation, for example, a significant fumble of a response during an important meeting; and/or c) an upcoming important presentation, which requires practice or preparation.

Scenario 'b' above refers to a typical impromptu speaking situation. Yet, few clients understand right off the bat the difference between a prepared speech or presentation or an impromptu one (*I tend to use 'prepared speech' and 'presentation' interchangeably here.)

So, I usually walk through different historicals and hypothetical scenarios to better inform my clients and understand their needs::

Scenarios

I'll often start off by asking new clients:

"Have you ever found yourself in an important meeting where, say, you are the subject expert in a certain area and an important stakeholder unexpectedly asks you for your opinion or recommendation on an issue? And you've got to come up with a compelling, coherent response right away?"

"Yes, that happens quite frequently."

"OK, great. That's a real-world example of an impromptu speaking situation."

I'll then often drill down further into their needs; very frequently, the client who believed they needed assistance with prepared presentations actually needs more assistance with impromptu speaking.

One of the most common issues my clients face in the meeting scenario described earlier is the feeling of being "at a loss for words" when put on the spot. They can thank the **'fight or flight' (acute stress)** response for that.

Our brains evolved to register threats in the environment, including physical threats. For whatever evolutionary reasons (or lack thereof), public speaking and public performances trigger a physical threat response in the participant.

Although the logical mind will tell us that no audience member will actually leap out and attack us as we speak, the subconscious and automatic mind perceive a potential threat; the linkage here is still unclear and buried deep in the more primitive parts of our minds.

As the acute stress response kicks in, voluntary cognitive functions can suffer, and the untrained speaker may forget what they planned to say. Instead, the speaker becomes hyper-aware of changes in their physiology and mind, which in turn can lead to a spiral of heightened anxiety.

THE IMPROMPTU SPEAKER'S TOOLKIT

It's a familiar scenario – a presenter is in a meeting or interview, and suddenly, all preparation goes out the window as the speaker struggles against the stress of the moment to articulate thoughts coherently.

As mentioned, I view presenting and public speaking as a cousin of the performative arts (performative arts include live theater, singing, and other affiliated forms). These performative areas are all subject to the fight or flight response to varying degrees.

I can still recall my very first Off-Off-Off Broadway theater performance in New York City over two decades ago: it was a bizarre and somewhat psychedelic kids show about an imaginary farm ruled by talking animals, in the vein of Sid and Marty Krofft.

The audience, consisting of kids and their parents, was very forgiving. No one cared about mistakes, or lines; indeed, many of the kids barely understood what the hell was going on. On a logical threat assessment level, the kids could not be a physical threat.

There was no *rational* reason to be afraid.

Yet I was terrified! My heart was racing, my palms were numb and clammy. I was held in the grips of the acute stress response, that fight or flight response which is hardwired into the most primitive areas of the human brain. I stood behind the curtain breathless, sweaty, with tunnel vision, waiting for my cue. I felt like running out of the theater while still wearing a full-body fox outfit.

Somehow, at the most agonizing peak of stress and doubt when my cue came, I was able to *physically* throw myself onto the stage for my entrance. Once committed in this way, the rest of the process (the show) became easier as the rational mind took over and the fight or flight response diminished.

My point is, **the uninitiated public speaker or presenter may not realize they are also engaged in a type of performative experience.** Having done both, I'm firmly convinced of this connection. The new speaker (or actor, or other performer) will likely sustain significant effects of the acute stress ('fight or flight') response at some point. This will lead to diminished cognitive flexibility, and, unless the participant has a firm mental template to hold onto throughout the process, they can stumble.

The effects of this acute stress response is further magnified in sudden, impromptu situations when there is no time to prepare, to stretch, to breath, to meditate, or to rehearse.

This is where impromptu speaking frameworks come into play. These are essentially *mental templates* that can be brought out rapidly and instinctively, for a range of scenarios.

The speaker's content is quickly then plugged into the various compartments of the framework, thus bypassing many of the problems associated with loss of cognitive dexterity during acute stress (fight or flight) scenarios.

What is Impromptu Speaking?

In contrast to planned presentations, **impromptu speeches** often occur spontaneously, with little on the spot preparation available. There may be only enough time for the speaker to hear the question, ingest its meaning, and then begin to formulate a response.

Impromptu speeches include, but are not limited to:

- Responding to questions during a business meeting
- Answering behavioral questions during a job interview
- Responding to lecturer's questions during an oral examination or discussion
- Summarizing the advantages and disadvantages of a situation
- Presenting a startup pitch
- Responding to questions in some social situations

An **extemporaneous speech** is similar to an impromptu speech, in that neither format is completely scripted. However, while both impromptu and extemporaneous speeches ditch the script, a key distinction sets them apart. *Impromptu speeches are truly off-the-cuff, and may be thrown at you with no prep time.* Extemporaneous speeches, on the other hand, offer a brief window of opportunity, as a speaker might have a few minutes to jot down some notes or mentally assemble some thoughts based on existing knowledge.

So let us once again refocus on impromptu speaking...

Examples

A classic example of an impromptu speech situation could be answering a sudden question during an all-hands meeting, with a speaker required to provide a compelling, coherent message immediately, without any preparation.

Another example could involve a student being asked a subject area question by an instructor in a group classroom environment.

In both cases, the speaker/presenter is required to respond to an inquiry with minimal on the spot preparation, without referencing notes or supporting materials. In both examples, a group of participant-onlookers is present, and the situation may be ripe for an acute stress (fight or flight) response.

Here are a few more examples:

The Surprise Q&A: You're at a conference, eagerly listening to a keynote speaker. As the presentation ends, the moderator announces a surprise Q&A session. Suddenly, you're called upon to share your thoughts on the speaker's message. With no time to prepare, you must articulate a thoughtful and relevant response.

<u>The Media Ambush:</u> You're a spokesperson for a company facing a PR crisis. A news reporter unexpectedly approaches you for a statement. With no time to consult your team or prepare a formal response, you must rely on your impromptu speaking skills to deliver a clear, concise, and reassuring message.

<u>The Classroom Challenge:</u> You're a student in a college class, and the professor suddenly calls on you to summarize the key points of the day's lecture. You haven't had a chance to review your notes, but you must quickly recall the information and present it coherently to the class.

Note that there is no time for *on the spot* preparation with an impromptu speech - *but this does not mean that there is 'no' preparation*. Preparation for impromptu speaking mainly takes the form of (to use movie production terminology) **pre-production**. That is: the impromptu speaker must anticipate contingencies in advance and prepare for those as thoroughly as is reasonably possible.

A speaker must, first and foremost, maintain the situational awareness to understand which environments and circumstances could require them to present an impromptu speech. Heading to a meeting where you are the subject area expert? You may be asked to deliver some informed opinions about your area of expertise, with little or no warning.

In addition to becoming intimately and instinctively

well-versed with several key frameworks, including those that appear in this resource, preparation for impromptu situations requires advance review of the subject area to be discussed and anticipation of likely or potential questions.

Benefits of Mastering Impromptu Speaking

Have you ever been caught off guard by a question or asked to speak on the spot? It can be nerve-wracking, but mastering impromptu speaking is a skill that can transform your personal and professional life. Not only does it help you navigate unexpected situations with confidence, but it also offers numerous benefits that can set you apart.

Let's delve into the specific advantages of honing this valuable skill:

- **Enhanced Credibility and Influence:** Demonstrating the ability to think on your feet and articulate your thoughts clearly under pressure establishes you as a credible and knowledgeable expert in your field. This can significantly boost your influence in professional and social settings.

- **Improved Adaptability and Agility:** Impromptu speaking forces you to think quickly and adapt to unexpected situations. This agility is a valuable asset in today's fast-paced world, where the ability to respond to change and uncertainty is crucial.

- **Increased Confidence and Self-Esteem:** Mastering impromptu speaking can be a significant confidence booster. As you become more comfortable speaking off the cuff, you'll develop a stronger sense of self-assuredness in your communication abilities.

- **Opportunities for Leadership:** Impromptu speaking skills are often associated with leadership qualities. When you can articulate your thoughts clearly and persuasively in the moment, you're more likely to be seen as a leader and decision-maker.

- **Career Advancement:** In many professions, the ability to speak eloquently and confidently without preparation is a highly sought-after skill. It can open doors to new opportunities, promotions, and career advancement.

It's Not a Conversation

Contrary to some perspectives, I would not classify impromptu presentations as a 'conversation' or 'conversational'. A conversation typically has no pre-set format, and relies heavily on interjections, slang, body language and informal speech devices to facilitate communication. A conversation involves a continuous feedback loop between two or more participants, versus

the speaker-centric arrangement found in even the most off-the-cuff impromptu speeches.

In a conversation, a speaker can simply ask questions (including hedging questions) in order to gain enough extra time and information to make some reasonable acceptable response, without the need for any efficient speaking mechanism. In a conversation, the speaker can and will quit their presentation on a whim, suddenly becoming a listener without needing to formulate or deliver any thesis or opinion at all. In a conversational environment, a speaker's presentation does not need to be compelling, or even factually true, just socially satisfying.

Finally, acute stress response (fight or flight) is less prevalent in conversational environments. Therefore, we can see that a conversation is much different than an impromptu presentation, and I would not equate the two.

In any case, an ability to deliver effectively in impromptu situations holds significant importance. Demonstrating quick thinking and adaptability lends credibility and influence in the eyes of peers, colleagues, and the community. In today's rapidly evolving work and academic landscapes, impromptu verbal communication skills often outweigh carefully planned speeches.

Impromptu speeches are vehicles to exert influence and persuasion. Leveraging these moments to motivate your teams can catalyze action more effectively. One's words can possess the power to instill confidence, to boost morale, and to enhance performance.

In times of crisis, impromptu speeches serve to reassure and lead teams, showcasing resilience and unwavering resolve.

Excelling in impromptu speaking, especially when under pressure, is a skill that can be honed through practice and employing effective strategies. It is often assumed that an effective impromptu speaker's main asset is an ability to think quickly on their feet. However, while an ability to improvise is useful, improvisation can't always be relied upon.

It is an impromptu speaker's preparatory discipline, in working with and practicing a range of effective frameworks, which ensures their success.

Impromptu Speaking vs. Conversation: *Summary of Key Differences*

Impromptu Speaking:

- Structured with clear beginning, middle, and end
- Purpose: To inform, persuade, or inspire

- Speaker's Role: Primary focus, delivers a prepared message
- Preparation: Relies on frameworks and pre-existing knowledge
- Psychological Impact: Can trigger acute stress response (fight or flight)

Conversation:

- Unstructured, free-flowing exchange
- Purpose: To build rapport, exchange information, socialize
- Speaker's Role: Equal participant, engages in back-and-forth dialogue
- Language: Informal, casual language, slang, and interjections
- Preparation: Minimal to no preparation
- Psychological Impact: Generally less stressful

What is a Framework?

A framework serves as a blueprint, aiding in the organization of a speaker's thoughts and arguments.

Essentially, a speaker will be 'plugging their thoughts' into the appropriate sections of a pre-made organizational template. This not only provides a clear structure for your message, but also acts as a safety net against the anxiety and "brain freeze" that often accompany impromptu speaking. By having a familiar structure to fall back on, a speaker can confidently navigate unexpected situations and deliver your message with clarity and conviction.

The template establishes a solid foundation for your message, akin to beams supporting a building during construction. An effective structure acts as the skeleton of your speech, ensuring coherence and logical flow.

Without it, your words may come across as disjointed and scattered. Moreover, even if aspects of your content or delivery falter, a robust structure enables your audience to follow along as you get back on track.

Two of the most effective frameworks for impromptu speaking are PREP (Point, Reason, Example, Point) and its modified variant, TREET (Thesis, Reason, Example, Example, Thesis).

PREP offers a straightforward approach, while TREET expands on this structure by incorporating two distinct examples to further support a claim or argument. We'll delve into these frameworks in more detail later, providing you with the tools to confidently tackle any impromptu speaking challenge.

Some new speakers may be skeptical of the practice of utilizing a framework in an ostensibly impromptu speaking environment. "A pre-made template? I don't want that, I want to think freely, to be in the moment, to think on my feet, and to present my own original thoughts and content."

My response is: in an impromptu speaking situation, with little time available, and adrenaline and cortisol flowing due to the acute stress (fight or flight) response, a speaker can't afford to risk fumbling around in the moment hoping to assemble their racing thoughts into a coherent message.

Unlike formal presentations, impromptu speaking is more likely to trigger a significant fight-or-flight response, leading to flustered and forgetful moments. So, a framework acts as a lifeline, offering a structured approach to organize thoughts amidst pressure.

You, as an emerging impromptu speaker, will need something reliable - a framework you are instinctively familiar with - in order to avoid scrambling to develop a message on the fly. Hence the frameworks below.

After you become very familiar with these frameworks (aka mental templates) and you become more experienced with impromptu speaking, you can modify these structures later as needed or desired. In fact, I created the TREET framework in 2023 as a modified variation of PREP specifically because I found many use cases where additional features were needed.

Bear in mind though, mere knowledge of any framework isn't sufficient. **They must be drilled and**

practiced until their use becomes second nature and instinctive.

For example, as a public speaking coach introducing a new framework to a client, we will typically spend half of the introductory session becoming familiar with the structure and terminology. This will be followed by 2-4 complete 90 minute sessions later just drilling and rehearsing the framework with a bank of questions which I gather and assemble in advance. The client is not aware of any of the questions in advance - this simulates actual impromptu speaking conditions.

The client will then use the appropriate framework (below) to formulate an effective response, again and again, over and over, for the next several sessions.

(By the way, If you would like to receive further coaching and rehearsal assistance in the use of these frameworks, contact me through linktr.ee/businessvoicecoach with any inquiries.)

In conclusion, a framework is not a constraint, but rather a powerful tool that empowers impromptu speakers. It provides a reliable structure amidst the chaos of unexpected situations, allowing your thoughts to flow smoothly and coherently. While some may initially hesitate to embrace a pre-made template, its benefits are undeniable. A framework serves as a safety net, preventing your message from unraveling under pressure. It enables you to focus on content delivery, confident in the knowledge that your structure is sound.

INTRODUCING: PREP & TREET

Useful in: Decision making meetings; brainstorming sessions; innovation meetings; dynamic and chaotic environments where time is limited; any situations where an impromptu speaker must make a coherent point quickly.

Imagine you are in an important meeting, with direct reports and various stakeholders present. You are the subject area expert in a certain department. The meeting is very dynamic and vocal: something important is being hammered out at this very moment, issues and procedures that will affect the direction of the whole organization.

Suddenly, a manager, direct report, or important stakeholder turns to you and asks:

"Well, [name], this is your area - what do you think we should do?"

Everyone turns to you…they are waiting for an answer.

A streamlined, compact, and efficient impromptu speaking framework would be very handy in the situation outlined above.

Enter the longstanding PREP method, and the contemporary modified variant, the TREET framework.

The exact origins of PREP are a bit difficult to pinpoint. Unlike some other public speaking frameworks with roots in ancient rhetoric, it seems to be a more modern invention, likely arising from communication training workshops and seminars.

Here's what we do know:

- **Focus on Simplicity:** The PREP method is valued for its straightforward structure (Point, Reason, Example, Point) making it easy to learn and remember, especially for those new to public speaking or facing impromptu situations.

- **Adaptability**: PREP can be modified as needed by experienced practitioners for upgraded performance. Hence the emergence of the TREET framework, which converts PREP's 'Point' to the term 'Thesis' instead, while prompting the speaker to include TWO examples, not just one (see more detailed explanations below)

- **Modern Communication Training:** The method is likely a product of 20th century communication training circles. Organizations like Toastmasters International, which started in 1924 and emphasizes clear and concise communication, likely played a role in popularizing the PREP approach.

THE IMPROMPTU SPEAKER'S TOOLKIT

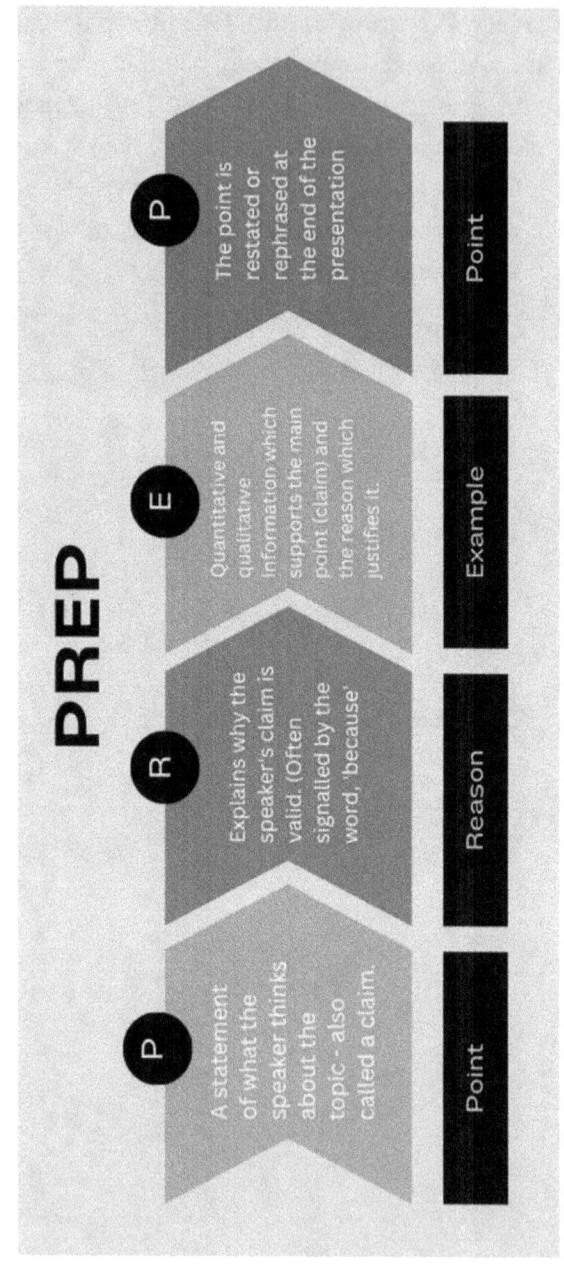

THE IMPROMPTU SPEAKER'S TOOLKIT

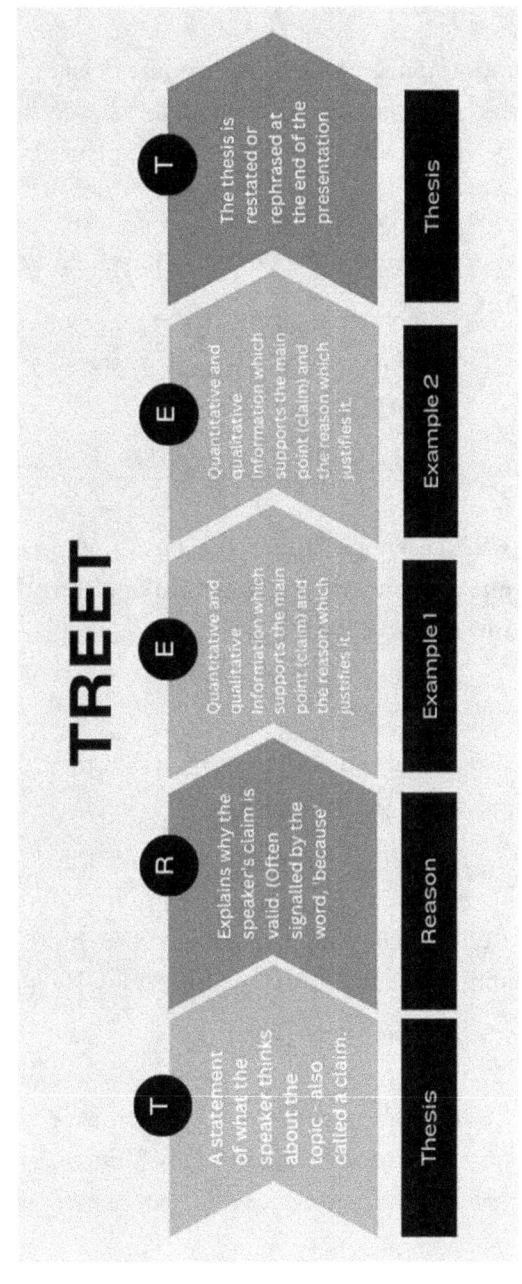

PREP & TREET in Action

PREP and TREET are both mnemonic devices, with each letter representing a component of the framework which the speaker must step through sequentially.

- The letters in PREP stand for 'Point - Reason - Example - (Restated) Point'
- The letters in TREET stand for 'Thesis - Reason - Example - Example - (Restated) Point'

Now let's examine the frameworks step by step:

Point (PREP) / aka Thesis (TREET): This is a statement of what the speaker thinks about the topic, and is also called a claim.

Good:

"Teenagers should be restricted in their gaming hours on school days"

"Cats are better pets than dogs."

"We should reduce operating costs by streamlining   our supply chain processes."

Poor:

"Cats are better than dogs. Except for huskies, and also we should consider Chihuahuas." (more than one claim, diffused/unclear claim)

> "Teenagers should be restricted in their gaming hours on school days. They also should be forced to wear ankle monitors. It's terrible being a teenager anyway." (more than one claim, irrelevant extra claim)

The speaker must promptly decide what their single most important claim is, and then stick to it. There is no time in a short impromptu presentation to discuss several possible claims, and doing so may cause confusion in the audience.

One of the most common problematic tendencies I've encountered when coaching new clients is when they seek to introduce an additional, secondary claim. With short form impromptu presentations, a speaker <u>must decide on one claim</u> and stick to it.

Reason: A reason is provided to explain why a claim is valid. This doesn't have to be stated as an opinion or prefaced with 'I think'; the claim and its reason can be stated as if factually true, for the sake of effective and persuasive rhetoric.

A reason is often (but not always) signaled with the word 'because'; if a speaker is in doubt as to where the reason may be placed for their claim, or how to phrase the reason, they may just lead out from their claim with the transitional word 'because", and this will naturally prompt their reason.

"Cats are better than dogs *because* they require less

maintenance." In this case, the claim is "Cats are better than dogs"; the reason for this claim is "they require less maintenance."

One of the most common errors I encounter when training a new speaker with PREP or TREET occurs when the speaker confuses the reason with examples, or skips the reason altogether and only provides examples without a reason:

Poor:

"Cats are better pets than dogs." (speaker accidentally skips the reason, and moves directly to example ->). "For example, an owner doesn't need to take their cat for a walk every day."

Good:

(Corrected example, with reason restored) "Cats are better pets than dogs, because they require less maintenance. For example, an owner doesn't need to take their cat for a walk every day."

Another error occurs when a speaker provides several reasons while using the TREET or PREP frameworks, when there should only be one. **In a short impromptu presentation, there can only be one reason for a claim** - basically because time and attention spans are limited.

Many speakers will have to fight the urge to provide additional reasons, but this is a discipline that's required in these short-form presentations. Providing an additional reason will a) confuse the audience, b) will diffuse the power of the overall presentation, and c) will chew up more time than may be available.

Poor:

"Cats are better than dogs, because they require less maintenance. They also are more beautiful overall." (Two reasons are given to explain the claim; we must stick to one overwhelming reason)

Good:

"Cats are better pets than dogs, because they require less maintenance." (The speaker decides on the single most compelling reason and sticks to it).

In longer, prepared presentations, multiple reasons may be given to support a claim. With this 'luxury' of additional time, an array of examples can be developed to support each reason. This level of development is just something not feasible in a short impromptu presentation using the PREP or TREET frameworks.

The speaker will provide supporting examples in the next step.

Example(s): Examples consist of quantitative and qualitative information which support the main point (claim) and the reason which justifies it.

The PREP framework does not specify what kind of

example or how many should be used; the TREET framework specifies two, with one being quantitative and the other qualitative (not necessarily in that order).

> **Quantitative examples feature quantitative data** - data which can be measured and quantified. This data can be counted, calculated, measured, and given a numerical value, i.e., number of users, percentage of earnings, and so forth. Quantitative data is structured after a research and/or evaluation process, and is used in analysis to bolster a claim.

Here is a quantitative example used to support a claim:

"Cats are better pets than dogs because they require less maintenance. (the claim) For example, 35% of cat owners state that they chose to own a cat instead of a dog because they didn't have time to walk a dog every day." (quantitative example using data from a survey).

> **Qualitative examples rely on qualitative data.** Qualitative data is used to categorize something in a descriptive way rather than with structured numerical data. Basically, qualitative data is information that can be seen, felt, or perceived. The data usually takes the form of testimony or anecdotes, provided by a user when describing their experience, or an observer of a situation.

Qualitative data is used by market researchers and

statisticians to understand behaviors, and it's often used by data analysts to understand and predict customer behavior. In an impromptu presentation, of course, qualitative data is used to formulate an example that supports a claim.

Quick stories or testimony may be used as a qualitative example, especially if the story is dramatic and/or the testimony comes from an expert, celebrity or powerful person.

Here is a quantitative example used to support a claim:

"Cats are better pets than dogs because they require less maintenance" (the claim) When I had dogs, they would often end up covered in smelly mud and thick burrs after running around outside. It took forever to clean them up afterwards." (qualitative examples using detailed first person testimony)

*Incidentally, I'd like to point out that I like dogs as well as cats, and the pro-cat claim here is just for reference and practice. Switch them around if you like!

A Deeper Dive into Examples:

The choice of quantitative or qualitative examples can be tailored to the audience and context for PREP and TREET.

PREP:

- **Audience: Data-Driven Professionals (Engineers, Analysts, etc.)**
    - **Context:** Presenting a proposal for a new software solution in a technical meeting.
    - **Example Type:** Quantitative. Focus on metrics like potential time savings, efficiency gains, or cost reductions backed by data. This resonates with their analytical mindset.

- **Audience: Sales Team**
    - **Context:** Motivational speech during a sales conference.
    - **Example Type:** Qualitative. Share inspiring success stories of individual sales reps or teams who exceeded targets, highlighting their dedication and strategies. This connects with their emotional drive and competitive spirit.

TREET:

- **Audience: Senior Management**
    - **Context:** Recommending a strategic investment in a new market.

- **Example Type:** Both Quantitative and Qualitative. Begin with quantitative data like market size, growth projections, and potential ROI. Follow up with qualitative examples, such as testimonials from satisfied customers in the new market or case studies of successful expansions by similar companies. This balanced approach appeals to both their logical and emotional decision-making processes.

- **Audience: Community Members**
    - **Context:** Town hall meeting to address concerns about a proposed development project.
    - **Example Type:** Both Quantitative and Qualitative. Start with qualitative examples like personal anecdotes or stories from community members affected by similar projects, showcasing the potential human impact. Then, present quantitative data on potential economic benefits, job creation, or environmental impact to provide a balanced perspective.

The choice between quantitative and qualitative examples is not always a binary decision. By understanding your audience's values, interests, and communication preferences, you can strategically choose the types of examples that will resonate most effectively and strengthen your impromptu presentation.

Point (PREP) / Thesis (TREET) - *Restated*. The speaker concludes their impromptu presentation by restating their Point (PREP) or Thesis (TREET). As a reminder, this is a repeat of the very first component that the speaker starts off with when making an initial claim. **Your audience will often remember your last words more than anything else.***

(*that is, if you make it that far in the presentation before being cut off or interrupted! Remember that TREET and PREP are often utilized in highly dynamic, sometimes chaotic environments with frequent interruptions and very limited time available)

In a brief impromptu presentation, the restated point or thesis can be similar to the initial one at the top of the presentation, if that's how it 'comes out'. If the speaker paraphrases and uses different words, that's even better.

But the goal is to avoid any fumbling around looking for words to paraphrase the initial claim, as there's no time to waste in delivering the impromptu presentation. The speaker may be lucky to arrive at this concluding stage at all - in very dynamic and chaotic speaking environments, interruptions by other speakers are likely and frequent.

In an ideal world, however, the impromptu speaker will step through all stages of the framework and deliver a repeat of the point / thesis as part of their initial claim.

One error I see frequently occurs when a speaker adds some totally new information in the conclusion of the framework.

No new information may be added at the end as an afterthought; it can confuse the audience and muddle the point. The speaker must remain disciplined by restating information already presented earlier in the initial claim.

Poor example of a conclusion using PREP or TREET

"Therefore it's clear that cats are better pets than dogs because they require less maintenance. Furthermore, they are simply more attractive overall." (This is a poor conclusion because the speaker introduced totally new information, an assessment of attractiveness, immediately following the restatement of the original Point/Thesis and Reason)

We can improve the conclusion simply by leaving off the extraneous information:

"Therefore it's clear that cats are better pets than dogs because they require less maintenance." (Point/Thesis + Reason)

"For this reason, I think we can all agree that cats are better pets than dogs." (Point/Thesis only without mentioning the Reason)

"To wrap up, cats are better pets than dogs" (Very basic but still workable)

Let's now look at the same sample presentation delivered with both PREP and TREET frameworks.

A speaker is asked for their opinion regarding the following question:

"How can we reduce operating costs without sacrificing product quality?"

> The speaker responds according to the PREP method: 'Point - Reason - Example - (Restated) Point'

Point: Streamlining supply chain processes.

> "We should reduce operating costs by streamlining supply chain processes…"

Reason: Efficiency gains lead to cost savings without compromising quality.

> "…because gains in efficiency will lead to cost savings without compromising quality"

Example: Implementing Just-In-Time inventory management to minimize excess inventory holding costs.

> "For example, one of our departments implemented a Just-in-Time inventory management system to minimize excess inventory holding costs."

Point (restated): Optimizing supply chain operations enables cost reduction while maintaining product standards.

> "Therefore, we should streamline our supply chain processes to reduce overall operating costs."

Summary: The impromptu speaker here first states their Point. The speaker then moves directly to the Reason; this is followed by an Example (presumably their best overall example), before wrapping up the presentation by restating the Point.

Compare this to a response using the modified TREET variant framework:

"How can we reduce operating costs without sacrificing product quality?"

> The speaker responds according to the TREET framework: 'Thesis - Reason - Example 1 - Example 2 - Thesis (Restated)'

Thesis: Streamlining supply chain processes.

"We can reduce operating costs by streamlining supply chain processes…"

Reason: Efficiency gains lead to cost savings without compromising quality.

> "...because gains in efficiency will lead to cost savings without compromising quality"

(Here's where TREET really differs from PREP...)

Example 1: *Quantitative* example regarding Just-In-Time inventory management to minimize excess inventory holding costs.

> "For example, one of our departments implemented a Just-in-Time inventory management system and reduced inventory holding costs by 15% year over year."

Example 2: *Qualitative* example regarding Just-In-Time inventory management to minimize excess inventory holding costs.

> "The head of that department said that the system was 'a breeze' to implement, and also presented end-user feedback ranging from 'very satisfied' to 'extremely satisfied' on followup surveys.

Thesis (Restated): Optimizing supply chain operations enables cost reduction while maintaining product standards.

> "Therefore, we should streamline our supply chain processes to reduce overall operating costs."

Summary: The impromptu speaker here first states their Thesis. The speaker then moves directly to the Reason; this is followed by Example 1 (Quantitative), then Example 2 (Qualitative), before wrapping up the presentation by restating the Thesis.

Analysis & Comparison

As seen with both frameworks, the speaker uses each letter of the name as a mnemonic prompt for formulating an efficient and coherent response. The speaker only needs to stick to the framework without wandering or ad-libbing, or the utility of the framework be lost.

We can see how the TREET Method differs from PREP in several key ways. In TREET, the introductory PREP component, 'Point', is replaced with a preferred academic writing term, 'Thesis', since a presenter's overall claim is more accurately identified as a thesis than a subsidiary point.

In academic writing and related areas, for instance, a *thesis statement* encapsulates the overarching theme, main idea, or purpose of the entire work, *whereas points* are specific assertions or claims made within the body of the spoken argument or text to support or elaborate on a thesis.

The concern is that an emerging speaker will confuse a single main point with their supporting examples. This is remedied by renaming the first step of the framework, from 'point' to 'thesis'.

Another greater difference between TREET and PREP is that TREET features *two* examples to support the thesis, not just one example (hence the two 'EEs' in TREET.)

A speaker could add several examples to a PREP delivery to extend it. However, a concern with that method's mnemonic device (one 'E' for one example) is that, in the heat of the moment and under stress, a speaker may unconsciously skip a second potential example in order to adhere to the strict letter of the framework.

A second example - if there is time and if it complements the first example effectively - can offer even more support to a point or thesis than a single example.

Another area of divergence is that the *types* of examples are more carefully specified in TREET than in PREP. The latter advises the use of 'an' example, but makes no mention whether the example included should be quantitative or qualitative. Rather than leave this up to guesswork, TREET directs the speaker to include one example of each type.

This formalization of example types and delivery is a modification that I added to the original PREP framework after much drilling and rehearsal of that approach with my clients. I noticed that some of them struggled in the moment to decide *what kind* of example to include to support their claim, which in turn caused them to hesitate in their delivery as they scrambled for one.

As a solution, I suggested that they include two examples: a quantitative example (a statistic, a number, a percentage etc.), which could generally appeal to audience members with a left-brained/logical orientation; and a quantitative example (a story, quoted testimony, etc.) which would appeal to listeners with a right-brained orientation.

It's understood that there is no absolute correlation between the type of example provided and any strict delineation between left and right brain types in the audience.

Sequencing of examples may be modified depending on the speaker's perceived demographic of the audience; if the audience is composed of data engineers, then I would suggest leading off with a quantitative example. On the other hand, if the presentation takes place in an emotionally driven or humanities-rich environment, then it may be suitable to lead off with a qualitative example.

Either way, the goal is to include two examples as a matter of process with the TREET method, or one example as specified with PREP.

Time is limited in an impromptu speaking environment.

Highly 'dynamic' or chaotic environments full of interruptions and alternating speakers may encroach on the impromptu speaker's presentation time, and delivery through the final restated point or thesis may not be possible if (or when) a speaker is cut off in mid-delivery.

Even so, both the PREP and TREET frameworks are designed to help formulate and successfully deliver a coherent and compelling presentation in the briefest time possible.

PRACTICE: PREP & TREET SAMPLE QUESTIONS & RESPONSES

The following sample questions and responses are best be utilized with a partner or coach; the trainee should not see the questions in advance, to best simulate an impromptu speaking scenario. Questions include a model response using both PREP and TREET for comparison purposes. The partner or coach should follow along and offer guidance if and when needed.

Note: it is often useful to record audio of speaker's responses for later review, using a smartphone app or dedicated device.

Question (Managerial) "How can we encourage more sustainable practices among our employees?"

PREP:

- **P (Point):** We should implement a comprehensive sustainability education program for all employees.

- **R (Reason):** Increased awareness and understanding of sustainability issues will lead to greater adoption of eco-friendly behaviors at work and at home.

- **E (Example):** A recent study by the Harvard Business Review found that companies with robust sustainability training programs saw a 25% reduction in energy consumption and a 15% decrease in waste generation within one year.

- **P (Point, restated):** Investing in sustainability education is not only good for the environment but can also lead to significant cost savings and improved employee morale.

TREET:

- **T (Thesis):** We should implement a comprehensive sustainability education program for all employees.

- **R (Reason):** Increased awareness and understanding of sustainability issues will lead to greater adoption of eco-friendly behaviors at work and at home.

- **E1 (Quantitative Example):** A recent study by the Harvard Business Review found that companies with robust sustainability training programs saw a 25% reduction in energy consumption and a 15% decrease in waste generation within one year.

- **E2 (Qualitative Example):** Employees who participated in a pilot sustainability program reported feeling more engaged with the company's values and a greater sense of personal responsibility for reducing their environmental impact.

- **T (Thesis, restated):** Investing in sustainability education is a win-win solution that benefits the environment, the company's bottom line, and employee satisfaction.

Question (from a Teacher): "In *To Kill a Mockingbird*, was Atticus Finch a good father? Why or why not?"

PREP:

- **P (Point):** Yes, Atticus Finch was a good father

- **R (Reason):** He instilled strong moral values in his children and taught them to stand up for what is right, even when it's unpopular.

- **E (Example):** When Scout is struggling to understand the racism in their community, Atticus encourages her to "climb into [someone else's] skin and walk around in it," fostering empathy and understanding.

- **P (Point, restated):** Despite the societal pressures of the time, Atticus Finch's unwavering commitment to justice and equality makes him an exemplary role model and a good father.

TREET:

- **T (Thesis):** Atticus Finch was a good father.

- **R (Reason):** He instilled strong moral values in his children and taught them to stand up for what is right, even when it's unpopular.

- **E1 (Quantitative Example):** Most students I surveyed believe that Atticus consistently models behaviors like fairness, respect, and integrity throughout the novel, setting a positive example for his children.

- **E2 (Qualitative Example):** When Jem destroys Mrs. Dubose's camellias in a fit of anger, Atticus makes him read to her as a way of teaching him about courage and understanding those who are different.

- **T (Thesis, restated):** Atticus Finch is a good father despite the challenges of his time.

(Community Meeting) "How can we improve community engagement in our local park clean-up initiatives?"

PREP:

- **P (Point):** We should organize a community-wide awareness campaign highlighting the benefits of a clean park.

- **R (Reason):** A clean park not only improves the aesthetic appeal of our neighborhood but also promotes health, safety, and community pride.

- **E (Example):** A similar initiative in a neighboring town led to a 30% increase in volunteer participation for park clean-up events

- **P (Point, restated):** By investing in a well-organized awareness campaign, we can increase community participation and ensure the long-term cleanliness and enjoyment of our local park.

TREET:

- **T (Thesis):** We should organize a community-wide awareness campaign highlighting the benefits of a clean park.

- **R (Reason):** A clean park not only improves the aesthetic appeal of our neighborhood but also promotes health, safety, and community pride.

- **E1 (Quantitative Example):** A survey conducted in a nearby community revealed that 85% of residents expressed greater willingness to participate in park clean-ups when they were aware of the positive impact on their community.

- **E2 (Qualitative Example):** Local businesses have expressed interest in sponsoring park clean-up events as a way to show their commitment to the community and attract customers.

- **T (Thesis, restated):** A multifaceted awareness campaign, supported by community partnerships, can significantly increase engagement in our park clean-up efforts and foster a stronger sense of community pride.

(Social Group Decision) "Where should we go for our weekend getaway?"

PREP:

- **P (Point):** We should go to the beach town of [Beach Town Name].

- **R (Reason):** It offers a relaxing atmosphere, beautiful scenery, and a variety of activities for everyone.

- **E (Example):** Last year, we had a fantastic time there swimming, sunbathing, and exploring the local shops and restaurants.

- **P (Point, restated):** [Beach Town Name] is the perfect destination for a fun and rejuvenating weekend escape.

TREET:

- **T (Thesis):** We should go to the beach town of [Beach Town Name].

- **R (Reason):** It offers a relaxing atmosphere, beautiful scenery, and a variety of activities for everyone.

- **E1 (Quantitative Example):** The town has a 95% satisfaction rating on travel websites, with many reviewers praising its cleanliness, friendly locals, and affordable accommodations.

- **E2 (Qualitative Example):** I've heard from several friends who have visited recently that the sunsets on [Beach Name] are absolutely breathtaking, and there's a vibrant nightlife scene with live music and dancing.

- **T (Thesis, restated):** With its stunning beaches, diverse activities, and rave reviews, [Beach Town Name] is the ideal choice for our weekend getaway.

School Board Meeting (Parent): "How can we improve communication between the school and parents?"

PREP:

- **P (Point):** We should implement a weekly email newsletter highlighting upcoming events,

  important announcements, and student achievements.

- **R (Reason):** A regular newsletter will keep parents informed and engaged with the school community, fostering a sense of transparency and collaboration.

- **E (Example):** A recent study by the National

PTA found that schools with regular communication channels like newsletters saw a 20% increase in parent involvement in school activities.

- **P (Point, restated):** A weekly newsletter is a simple yet effective way to bridge the communication gap between the school and parents, leading to greater involvement and support for our students.

TREET:

Question (Parent): "How can we improve communication between the school and parents?"

- **T (Thesis):** We should implement a weekly email newsletter highlighting upcoming events, important announcements, and student achievements.

- **R (Reason):** A regular newsletter will keep parents informed and engaged with the school community, fostering a sense of transparency and collaboration.

- **E1 (Quantitative Example):** A survey of parents in our district revealed that 75% feel they are not receiving enough information about school activities and events.

- **E2 (Qualitative Example):** Many parents have

expressed a desire for more frequent and detailed updates about their children's progress in school, as well as upcoming deadlines and opportunities.

- **T (Thesis, restated):** By establishing a consistent communication channel like a weekly newsletter, we can address parent concerns, increase transparency, and strengthen the partnership between home and school.

(Marketing Director) "Our company's website is experiencing high bounce rates. What can we do to improve visitor engagement?"

PREP:

- **P (Point):** We should prioritize a complete redesign of the website's user interface (UI) and user experience (UX).

- **R (Reason):** A more intuitive, visually appealing, and user-friendly website will encourage visitors to stay longer and explore our products and services.

- **E (Example):** A study by Forrester Research revealed that a well-designed UX can yield conversion rates up to 400%, demonstrating the significant impact of user-centric design on business outcomes.

- **P (Point, restated):** Investing in a website redesign focused on UI/UX will not only reduce bounce rates but also enhance our brand image and ultimately drive more leads and sales.

TREET:

- **T (Thesis):** We should prioritize a complete redesign of the website's user interface (UI) and user experience (UX).

- **R (Reason):** A more intuitive, visually appealing, and user-friendly website will encourage visitors to stay longer and explore our products and services.

- **E1 (Quantitative Example):** Studies have shown that websites with strong UI/UX design can increase visitor engagement by up to 200% and lead to a 400% increase in conversion rates.

- **E2 (Qualitative Example):** User feedback on our current website often mentions confusing navigation, slow loading times, and a lack of visual appeal. A redesign can address these issues and create a more positive impression of our brand.

- **T (Thesis, restated):** By investing in a well-designed UI/UX, we can create a website that not only attracts visitors but also keeps them engaged, ultimately driving more leads and sales.

(Human Resource Manager) "Should our company adopt a permanent remote work policy?"

PREP:

- **P (Point):** Yes, we should transition to a permanent remote work model.

- **R (Reason):** Embracing remote work offers numerous benefits, including increased employee satisfaction, reduced overhead costs, and access to a wider talent pool.

- **E (Example):** A recent survey by FlexJobs revealed that 76% of employees would be more likely to stay with their current employer if they could work remotely, highlighting the potential impact on retention.

- **P (Point, restated):** Adopting a permanent remote work policy is a forward-thinking strategy that can boost employee morale, productivity, and overall company performance.

TREET:

- **T (Thesis):** Yes, we should transition to a permanent remote work model.

- **R (Reason):** Embracing remote work offers numerous benefits, including increased employee satisfaction, reduced overhead costs, and access to a wider talent pool

- **E1 (Quantitative Example):** Global Workplace Analytics estimates that companies can save an average of $11,000 per year for every employee who works remotely half of the time.

- **E2 (Qualitative Example):** Many employees have reported improved work-life balance, reduced commute stress, and increased focus when working from home.

- **T (Thesis, restated):** Embracing remote work is a strategic move that can lead to cost savings, happier employees, and ultimately, a more successful company.

Public Debate (Moderator): "Should the voting age be lowered to 16?"

PREP:

- **P (Point):** Yes, the voting age should be lowered to 16.

- **R (Reason):** Young people at this age are capable of making informed decisions and should have a say in the issues that affect their future.

- **E (Example):** Countries like Austria and Scotland have successfully lowered the voting age to 16, resulting in increased youth engagement in politics and higher voter turnout.

- **P (Point, restated):** Lowering the voting age to 16 is a step towards a more inclusive and representative democracy.

TREET:

- **T (Thesis):** Yes, the voting age should be lowered to 16.

- **R (Reason):** Young people at this age are capable of making informed decisions and should have a say in the issues that affect their future.

- **E1 (Quantitative Example):** Studies show that 16- and 17-year-olds possess similar levels of civic knowledge and political understanding as older voters.

- **E2 (Qualitative Example):** Many young people are passionate about social and environmental issues and have demonstrated their ability to organize and advocate for change.

- **T (Thesis, restated):** Empowering 16- and 17-year-olds with the right to vote is a crucial step towards a more just and equitable society.

After working through these questions, both coach and speaker will have a much better idea about developing further original question-response material.

Try to formulate 50-100 new questions based on a range of topics, including subject area expertise of the speaker.

RECAP

The TREET & PREP methods are impromptu speaking frameworks for use in business meetings, group discussions, and similar environments where a speaker must deliver a well formulated and compelling response succinctly and with minimal (or no) preparation.

These frameworks are best applied to situations where time is limited and the speaker must make a strong claim ('Thesis' or 'Point') from the very beginning.

- TREET stands for Thesis, Reason, Example 1, Example 2, and Thesis (Restated)

- PREP stands for Point, Reason, Example, and Point (Restated)

- Both of these frameworks are mnemonic devices which assist a speaker by providing a template for a brief and compelling impromptu presentation. The speaker recalls each letter of their chosen framework and insert their spoken content according to each cue.

- TREET and PREP differ in some of their basic terminology, and number (and type) of recommended examples required.

THE IMPROMPTU SPEAKER'S TOOLKIT

- Use either or both frameworks as needed - try them out and drill them both to determine your preference.

Feature	**PREP**	**TREET**
Acronym	Point, Reason, Example, (Restated) Point	Thesis, Reason, Example, Example, (Restated) Thesis
Focus	Single main point	Thesis statement as central argument
Examples	One example	Two examples (quantitative & qualitative)
Simplicity	Easier to learn and remember	Slightly more complex but offers greater depth
Flexibility	Can be adapted, but less structured	More structured, guides example selection

Ideal Use Cases	Quick responses, limited time	Slightly longer responses, opportunity for nuance

PREP Advantages:

- **Simplicity:** Easy to learn and remember, ideal for beginners or those under pressure.

- **Adaptability:** Can be modified to fit various situations and extended with additional examples if time allows.

- **Conciseness:** Delivers a clear and focused message quickly.

PREP Disadvantages:

- **Limited Depth:** Only one example may not be enough to fully support the point in some situations.

- **Less Guidance:** Does not specify the type of example to use, which may lead to hesitation or less impactful choices.

- **Potential Oversimplification:** May not be suitable for complex topics that require more nuanced arguments.

TREET Advantages:

- **Depth and Nuance:** Two examples (quantitative and qualitative) provide stronger evidence and appeal to diverse audiences.

- **Structured Approach:** Guides the speaker to include both types of evidence, reducing hesitation and ensuring a well-rounded argument.

- **Persuasiveness:** The combination of data and personal stories can be more convincing than a single example.

TREET Disadvantages:

- **Slightly More Complex:** Requires a bit more practice to master compared to PREP.

- **Time Constraints:** May not be suitable for very short time frames where only one example is feasible.

- **Potential Over-reliance on Structure:** Might hinder creativity and spontaneity for experienced speakers.

ACTION STEPS FOR THE EMERGING SPEAKER

Find a Coach or Practice Partner: Seek out a qualified coach or a trusted friend or colleague to review and practice the TREET and/or PREP frameworks. I specialize in coaching both frameworks (I created the TREET model in 2023 as an enhanced version of PREP) and can offer extensive experience guiding clients to success with this and other frameworks, if I'm available. Contact: **linktr.ee/businessvoicecoach**

Create a Question Bank: Collaborate with your coach or partner to create a diverse bank of questions, encompassing both your field of expertise and general topics. Remember, the element of surprise is key to simulating real-world impromptu scenarios.

Drill the Frameworks: Engage in multiple practice sessions, dedicating at least several 90-minute sessions to drilling the frameworks until their use becomes automatic and instinctive. This is often the most underestimated step, but it's absolutely crucial for mastery.

Seek Immediate Feedback: Encourage your coach or partner to provide immediate feedback and error correction after each practice round. This will help you identify areas for improvement and refine your technique.

Practice in Real-Life Scenarios: Look for opportunities to apply the frameworks in real-world situations. This could involve participating in workplace discussions, community meetings, social gatherings, or even online forums.

Mirror Practice: Stand in front of a mirror and practice responding to impromptu questions using the frameworks. Pay attention to your body language, facial expressions, and overall delivery.

Record and Review: Record yourself practicing with the frameworks. Analyze the recordings to identify areas where you can improve your clarity, conciseness, and persuasiveness.

Did you know?

A longer, more comprehensive impromptu speech can be crafted by linking a series of TREET or PREP presentations together! This modular approach allows you to tackle complex topics, offering multiple points or theses with supporting evidence while still maintaining a clear and organized structure.

For example, imagine you're asked to give an impromptu presentation on "How to Improve Employee Morale." You could break this broad topic down into several smaller TREET presentations:

1. **TREET 1:** Focus on the importance of recognition and rewards (as seen in the earlier example).

2. **TREET 2:** Discuss the benefits of a flexible work environment, citing studies on increased productivity and reduced stress.

3. **TREET 3:** Emphasize the importance of professional development opportunities, sharing examples of how training programs have boosted morale and retention rates.

By linking these TREET presentations together with brief transitions, you create a well-rounded impromptu speech that addresses multiple facets of the issue while maintaining a clear structure and delivering a compelling message.

This technique also works well with the PREP framework. You can link multiple points together, each supported by its own reason and example, to create a more comprehensive argument.

The key is to ensure that each individual TREET or PREP presentation stands alone as a coherent argument, while also contributing to the overall message of your impromptu speech. By mastering this technique, you'll be able to confidently tackle even the most challenging impromptu speaking scenarios.

CONCLUSION

In the unpredictable landscape of modern communication, impromptu speaking skills have become more essential than ever. Whether you're in a boardroom, a classroom, or a social gathering, the ability to articulate your thoughts clearly and persuasively on the spot can be a game-changer.

The PREP and TREET frameworks, as detailed in this guide, offer structured approaches to navigate these spontaneous speaking situations with confidence.

I believe the PREP and TREET frameworks are effective ways to give short impromptu presentations because they provide a handy mnemonic device to follow in step by step fashion as a speaker delivers their message. This helps to bypass, or at least reduce, the effects of acute stress response (fight or flight) which can obstruct a speaker's performance.

By mastering these tools and practicing consistently, you can develop the agility, credibility, and influence that are hallmarks of effective impromptu speakers.

Remember, the key to success lies in preparation. Familiarize yourself with the frameworks, practice them diligently, and seek feedback from trusted mentors, coaches, or peers. The more you practice, the more natural and instinctive these frameworks will become, allowing you to effortlessly respond to any unexpected question or challenge.

These frameworks are useful in: decision-making meetings; brainstorming sessions; innovation meetings; a dynamic and chaotic environment where time is limited; and any situation where an impromptu speaker must make a coherent point quickly.

As you embark on your journey to becoming a skilled impromptu speaker, remember that it's not about perfection but about progress. Embrace the learning process, experiment with different approaches, and tailor your delivery to suit your audience and context. With dedication and perseverance, you can unlock the full potential of your voice and become a truly impactful communicator.

Best of Luck on Your Impromptu Speaking Journey!

Jason Rosette

ABOUT THE AUTHOR

Jason Rosette is an award winning writer-director, public speaking coach, and educator with over three decades experience working in the USA and abroad.

A graduate of NYU Film (BFA), with an MA in International Development studies from Royal University of Phnom Penh, Jason Rosette self-launched his career in New York with the feature documentary, 'BookWars' ("Terrific" - LA Times). The movie was screened and broadcast widely, and is now a part of the circulating films collection at the Museum of Modern Art in New York.

He began coaching public speaking in 2019, as an extension of his directing and coaching talent in the performing arts. He now works in both areas, seeing significant useful and interesting overlap between them.

Jason is also a narrator of audiobooks, and a producer of long form audio, music and related media. Visit Audible, Apple Music, Spotify, and other platforms for a brief list of affiliated titles.